LIVES
AND
TIMES

Diana, Princess of Wales

Haydn Middleton

Heinemann
LIBRARY

First published in Great Britain by Heinemann Library
Halley Court, Jordan Hill, Oxford OX2 8EJ,
a division of Reed Educational and Professional Publishing Ltd.
Heinemann is a registered trademark of Reed Educational & Professional Publishing Limited.

OXFORD FLORENCE PRAGUE MADRID ATHENS
MELBOURNE AUCKLAND KUALA LUMPUR SINGAPORE TOKYO
IBADAN NAIROBI KAMPALA JOHANNESBURG GABORONE
PORTSMOUTH NH (USA) CHICAGO MEXICO CITY SAO PAULO

Designed by Ken Vail Graphic Design, Cambridge
Illustrations by Oxford Illustrators
Printed and bound in Italy by Lego

02 01 00 99 98
10 9 8 7 6 5 4 3 2 1

ISBN 0 431 02506 1

Some words are shown in bold, **like this**. You can find out what they mean by looking in the glossary. The glossary also helps you say difficult words.

British Library Cataloguing in Publication Data

Middleton, Haydn
Diana, Princess of Wales. - (Lives & times)
1. Diana, Princess of Wales - Juvenile literature
2. Princesses - Great Britain - Biography - Juvenile literature
I. Title
941' .085'092

Acknowledgements

The Publishers would like to thank the following for permission to reproduce photographs:

Chris Honeywell pp17, 21, 22; Remember When p16, reproduced with permission of Mirror Group Newspapers; Rex Features p19, T Rooke p18, P Brooker p20; Sygma/M Polak p23

Cover photograph reproduced with the permission of Pool, Camera Press.

Every effort has been made to contact copyright holders of any material reproduced in this book. Any omissions will be rectified in subsequent printings if notice is given to the Publisher.

All royalties from the sale of this book go to the Diana, Princess of Wales Memorial Fund.

Contents

The first part of this book tells you the story of
Diana, Princess of Wales.
The second part tells you how you can find out
about her life.

Early life

Diana Spencer was born in 1961. Her family was very rich and lived in a big country house. When she was a girl she sometimes played with Queen Elizabeth's children.

When Diana left school, she got a job in London. She helped to look after young children at a **kindergarten**.

Joining the royal family

When Diana was 19 years old, Prince Charles, Queen Elizabeth's oldest son, asked her to marry him. Diana said yes. Charles was called the **Prince of Wales**. Diana would become the Princess of Wales.

The wedding was in London on 29 July 1981.
People all over the world watched it on
television. Some people thought Diana was
like a princess from a fairytale.

Meeting the people

Wherever Diana went with Prince Charles, people wanted to see her. She was friendly and kind to everyone. 'She's just like one of us,' people would say.

Sons

In 1982 Diana had a baby son, William.
In 1984 she had a second son, Harry.
When Queen Elizabeth dies, Prince
Charles will become king. When Charles
dies, William will become king.

Giving help

Diana was very good at **raising money** for people who were old, poor or sick. Most of all, she enjoyed helping children.

Diana visited hospital patients in many different countries. She said that she wanted to be 'a princess for the world'.

World-famous

People liked to read about all the things Diana did. Sometimes the newspaper **reporters** and photographers **pestered** Diana too much.

This made her unhappy. Also, she was not getting on well with Prince Charles. In 1996 they were **divorced**.

A sad death

On 31 August 1997, Diana was killed in a car crash in Paris. She was only 36 years old. Many thousands of people went to put flowers outside her home.

There were more than a million **mourners** at her **funeral**. No member of the royal family had ever been so popular.

Newspapers and books

There are many ways for us to find out about Diana. From 1981 to 1997, stories about her were printed in the newspapers. Special libraries keep copies of old newspapers for us to look at.

Lots of books about Diana were **published** when she was alive. This book was published in 1992. Diana and her friends told the writer all about her life.

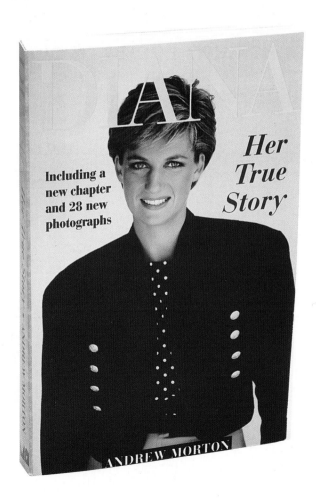

Film and photos

Television crews often filmed Diana on her travels. We can watch the films to find out how Diana looked and talked. Here she is meeting people in Bosnia, in 1997, where there had been a war.

Photographers even took photos of Diana when she was relaxing or on holiday. This made her angry. This photo shows her hiding from photographers with her son, Harry.

Tributes

When Diana died, even people who had never met her felt very sad. They gave **tributes** to show their **respect** for her. This card was fixed to a bunch of flowers.

"Princess Diana"

"The flowers"

"I give flowers, I love Princess Diana"
love Syeda
Sye 6
X   X

"I know that dead, but th will touch
Emil

The pop star, Elton John, played a tribute song to Diana at her **funeral**. It was called *Candle in the Wind*. He recorded the song. Millions of people bought it and most of the money went to **charity**.

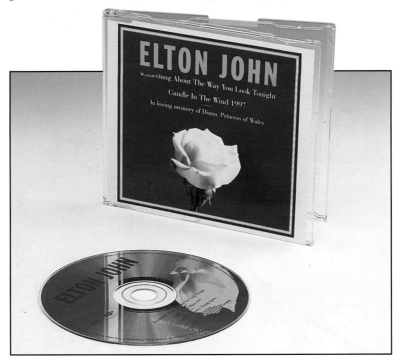

Souvenirs

Diana was very popular, so people liked to collect things with her picture on. In 1981, when she was married to Prince Charles, you could buy mugs and books like these.

Grave

You can visit Diana's childhood home at Althorp, Northamptonshire. Her grave is on this tiny island in the grounds of the house.

Glossary

This glossary explains difficult words and tells you how to say words which are hard to read.

charities groups of workers who help people in need.
You say *cha-ri-tiz*

divorced stopped being married

funeral the church service which celebrates the life of someone who has died

kindergarten a school for very little children.
You say *kin-de-gar-ten*

mourners people who are sad when someone dies.
You say *mor-ners*

pestered bothered

Prince of Wales the oldest son of the British king or queen. Wales is in Britain

published printed and put on sale

raising money getting people to give money to help those in need

reporters people who write in newspapers or speak about news on television

respect to value someone and look up to them

tributes things that are said, written or done, to show how much someone means to you.
You say *trib-youts*

Index